MICROCRAFTS

Tiny Treasures to Make and Share

Compiled by

Margaret McGuire, Alicia Kachmar, Katie Hatz
and Friends

QUIRK BOOKS

PHILADELPHIA

A Very Big Thank-You

To our photographer Steve Belkowitz, without whose
care and patience we never would have gotten the
perfect shot of Rory the rabbit's hindquarters.

♥

Copyright © 2011 by Quirk Productions, Inc.

All artwork courtesy and copyright of individual designers or design studios.

Library of Congress Cataloging in Publication Number: 2011922693

ISBN: 978-1-59474-521-8

Printed in China

Typeset in Cochin, Eureka, and Eureka Sans

Designed by Katie Hatz
Photographs by Steve Belkowitz except page 13 by Nadia Marks Wojcik,
and pages 86 and 87 submitted by authors.
Production management by John J. McGurk

Quirk Books
215 Church Street
Philadelphia, PA 19106
quirkbooks.com

10 9 8 7 6 5 4 3 2 1

Small is beautiful.

CONTENTS

Introduction 1

How to Use This Book 3

Boats 5

Books 7

Bottle-Cap Frames 11

Bunting 13

Candy Charms 15

Cats 19

Deer Heads 21

Dogs 25

Fabric Buttons 31

Flower Pocket Pendants 33

Greeting Cards 37

Houseplants and Terrariums 43

Ladybugs, Bumblebees, and
   Butterflies 47

Monster Babies 49

Owls 53

Party Hats 55

Planets 59

Porcupine and Friends 61

Ribbon Bows 63

Speech Bubbles 65

Spool Dolls 67

Teddy Bears 69

Temporary Tattoos 73

Thistle Birdfeeders 75

Yellow Polka Dot Bikini 77

Supplies and Techniques 81

Ideas for Modifying Microcrafts 84

Resources 85

About the Authors 86

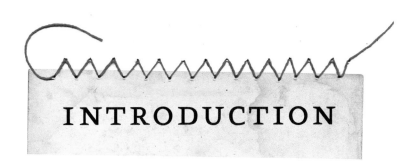

INTRODUCTION

Hello!

If you're reading this book, chances are you already have a minor obsession with adorably tiny trinkets and treasures. But microcrafting isn't just about a love of all things small. It's really all about putting odds and ends to good use.

How to Use This Book

In this book, you'll find twenty-five miniature craft projects that use a variety of different methods and materials. Most of these projects are meant to be fairly quick and easy, whether you've got two left thumbs or years of experience. It doesn't take much to get started microcrafting. All you need is a few odds and ends and some everyday tools and supplies (see page 81). Oh, and maybe a good pair of glasses.

Each craft is tagged with its real-life size and its designer's name, followed by easy illustrated instructions, traceable patterns, and tips and tricks for working in a wee format. And all of the projects leave room for your own interpretations and modifications.
Once you learn the basics, there are endless ways to adapt these instructions. "Ideas for Modifying Microcrafts" (page 84) is just the tip of the (mini) iceberg: We hope you'll use this book as inspiration for creating your own small-scale designs. Visit quirkbooks.com/microcrafts for extra downloadables and advice, and to share your miniature creations with us.

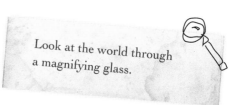

Look at the world through a magnifying glass.

Actual size: About 1 inch
long, depending on the nut
Designed by: Alicia Kachmar

BOATS

Row, row, row your . . . peanut? Petite boats that truly float can be made from the shells of walnuts, almonds, peanuts, or pistachios. Equip them with a simple mast and you're ready to set sail.

SUPPLIES

assorted shelled nuts

nutcracker or pliers

toothpicks

scissors

leaves

craft glue

Any leaf—dried or fresh—will do; just be gentle if the foliage is brittle or delicate.

1 **Gently crack open a nutshell** using a nutcracker or pliers. Place half of the empty shell on a flat surface, open side up.

2 **To make the mast,** trim a toothpick to about 1 inch. (Any taller, and your little ship will likely capsize.) Insert the toothpick's pointy end at the bottom of a leaf, from front to back. Then poke the toothpick back through at the top, curving the leaf like a sail.

3 **Place a small amount of glue** in the bottom of the shell and put the cut end of the toothpick in the glue. Hold the toothpick in place or prop it against something while the glue dries. Make as many little boats as you like and then set off to sea.

Trim ends off 2 toothpicks or matchsticks to make oars for peanut rowboats. Attached with a dab of glue, they help little boats stay afloat.

Actual size: 1 by 1¼ inches
Designed by: Melissa Jacobson

BOOKS

With paper odds and ends, you can make miniature books to display
on your bookshelves or give to your friends.

SUPPLIES

1 8-by-5¾-in sheet of office paper

craft knife and cutting mat

ruler

2 1¾-by-1⅛-in sheets of decorative paper

1 1-by-1⅛-in sheet of scrap paper

foam *or* cardboard scrap

awl *or* sturdy pushpin

nylon thread and embroidery needle

1 2-by-1¼-in (at least) piece of thick card
 stock *or* thin board

craft glue

1 2¾-by-1¾-in sheet of decorative paper
 (for the cover)

wax paper scraps (optional)

2 **Make the endpapers** by folding the 2 1¾-by-1 ⅛-inch decorative papers in half, matching the size of the ⅞-by-1⅛-inch signatures. These endpapers will attach to the inside of the cover.

3 **Make a sewing template** (for binding the book) by folding the scrap paper in half to measure ½ by 1⅛ inches. Open the paper and lay it on foam or cardboard. Using an awl or pushpin, punch 5 holes in the fold. (Mark the top with a pencil so you know which way is up.) Use the template and the awl to punch 5 holes into the fold of each signature and endpaper. Keep track of the top of each so that the holes align when you sew everything together.

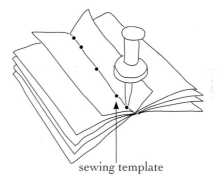

sewing template

4 **Make the book block** by aligning and sewing together the endpapers and signatures, following the numerical order shown in the diagram (see next page). Note that solid lines indicate stitches outside the folded edge (spine), and dotted lines indicate stitches inside the fold. Knot the thread at the end of the stitches to secure.

1 **Make the book's interior** by folding the 8-by-5¾-inch office paper 3 times. Trim the unfolded edge to ⅞ inch wide. Cut the remaining piece widthwise into 5 sections that are each ⅞ by 1⅛ inches; these will be the signatures, or groups of pages in the book. When folded, each signature will have 16 pages, or 8 leaves.

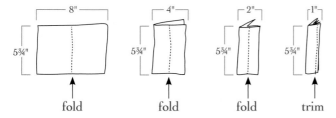

Avoid embroidery thread and traditional bookbinding threads. They're too thick and likely to tangle.

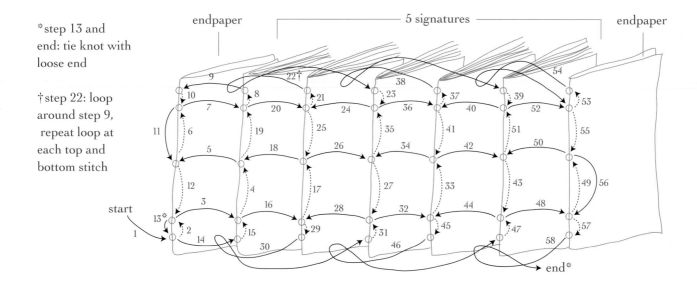

*step 13 and
end: tie knot with
loose end

†step 22: loop
around step 9,
repeat loop at
each top and
bottom stitch

endpaper

5 signatures

endpaper

start

5 **Make the cover** by cutting the card stock into 3 pieces to fit the front, spine, and back of the book block. Glue the pieces to the wrong (back) side of the 2¾-by-1¾-inch decorative paper, leaving a very small space between them, as shown. After the glue dries, trim the corners of the paper, leaving enough to fold over the card stock. Apply a small amount of glue around the edges of the paper and fold it over the card stock, tucking the corners in.

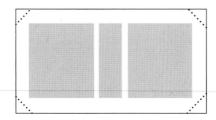

trim the cover's corners

6 **Glue the cover** to the endpapers on the outside of the book block. Press the book under a heavy object (we recommend *Merriam-Webster's Collegiate Dictionary, 11th Edition*). To prevent glue from seeping onto the book's pages, place wax paper between the inside covers and endpapers.

7 **To add a belly band** like the turquoise one on page 6, cut a ⅛-inch slit ¼ inch from the bottom edge of a ¼-by-2¾-inch strip of decorative paper. Wrap the belly band tightly around your finished book, mark where the slit touches the opposite end of the strip, and cut a

⅛-inch slit from the top edge at this point. Now wrap the belly band around your book and slide the two slits into each other to fasten.

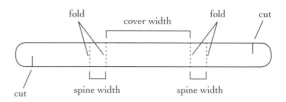

belly band

Clockwise from lower left: loose signatures, assembled book block, and a book cover almost ready to be glued to the book block.

Scale this project down to make tiny volumes only a bookworm could read. For directions on attaching jump rings to turn microcrafts into wearable art, see page 84.

Actual size: 1 inch in diameter
Designed by: Tamara Barker

BOTTLE-CAP FRAMES

Have you ever wanted to print your own picture on the inside of a bottle cap? Follow these instructions to frame anything from hand-lettered notes to magazine tear outs, drawings, and vintage photographs.

SUPPLIES

a favorite image
card stock
clear packing tape
metal bottle cap
hand punch *or* hammer and awl/nail
craft glue
8- to 10-mm jump ring
necklace chain
needle-nose pliers
magnet *or* earring-post blanks

1 **Select a special image to frame.** If using a digital image, use photo-editing software to size it to the diameter of your bottle cap. Print it on card stock and trim around the image.

2 **Seal the image** by covering the front and back with a protective layer of clear packing tape.

3 **Make a hole in the center** of the top ridge of the bottle cap, using the hand punch or hammer and nail. (If you're making a magnet or post earrings, skip this step.) When punching metal, watch out for your fingers, and file down sharp edges around the hole.

4 **Glue the image into the bottle cap.** Allow to dry completely.

5 **Turn your frame into a charm** by adding a jump ring. Use pliers to loop the jump ring through the hole in the cap; now you can easily thread it onto a necklace, earring wire, or key chain. Alternatively, you can apply glue to the back of the bottle cap and adhere it to something flat, like a magnet or earring post.

Punches make quick work of cutting neat paper dots and piercing holes into metal. A 1-inch circular punch works best for paper; a 1/16-inch hand punch is great for bottle caps.

Scan these or resize any digital picture to 1 inch in diameter to fit the bottle cap.

Actual size: Varies
Designed by: Nadia Marks Wojcik

BUNTING

Personalizing a cake, cupcakes, or any tasty treat just got a whole lot cuter—and easier. You don't even have to be a master with the frosting tube. Just try some simple paper-crafting for a one-of-a-kind embellishment.

SUPPLIES

scraps of card stock in assorted colors

scissors

sewing machine *or* embroidery needle and thread

bamboo skewers

hot glue gun

When sewing together the triangles, be sure to leave long tails of thread at each end for tying onto the bamboo skewers.

1 **Cut the card stock** into 1-inch strips. Next, make triangles that are about ¾ inch at the base by cutting back and forth at an angle down the length of each strip.

cut 1-inch strips into triangles

Skip the bamboo skewers for bunting that you want to hang on the wall or in a window.

2 **Stitch together the triangles** using a sewing machine, feeding them individually. Sew as many triangles as desired, making a bunting that is 1 inch longer than the distance between the skewers when placed in the cake. (For example, a 6-inch-wide cake requires 5 inches of bunting if the skewers are placed 4 inches apart).

3 **Lay the bunting on a flat surface** and wrap one end of the thread several times around the dull end of a skewer. Hold the thread taut and put a thin line of hot glue over the wrapped threads; allow to dry. Repeat with the other skewer.

Actual size: ⅓ inch
Designed by: Mei Pak

CANDY CHARMS

Who doesn't have a sweet tooth? Decorate bracelets, necklaces, and more with these make-and-bake cupcakes, lollipops, and chocolates. Once you get used to working with polymer clay, it's easy to create your own microfood designs.

SUPPLIES

blobs of polymer clay in a few colors

craft knife

eye pins

wire cutter

clear nail polish

bonding glue (optional)

Cupcake

1. **Make the base** by rolling a clay ball into an egg shape. Cut off the thicker end by sawing gently with the craft knife while rotating the clay, applying equal pressure all around. Use the blade's blunt side to lightly press lines around the circumference of the base to make ridges, like those on cupcake papers.

2. **Make the frosting** by rolling a second ball of clay into a thin log. Place one end in the center of the cupcake's top, curling outward to the edge. Wrap the log around the cupcake's top, making consecutively smaller circles. Cut off excess clay.

press   coil

3. **Use a wire cutter to cut an eye pin** to the length of the cupcake and insert it in the middle.

4. **Bake according to the directions** on the polymer clay package. Allow to cool. Coat with clear nail polish and allow to dry. Note that, after baking, you can remove the eye pin, dip it in strong bonding glue, and reinsert it.

Lollipop

1. **Roll a ball of clay** into a thick log. Loop it around another ball of clay, cut off the excess, and loop it around again to make a cross. Gently roll to blend the colors and make a log, then twist to swirl the colors. Roll up the log to make a coil.

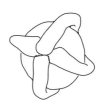   

wrap and then roll   trim the coil

2. **Make the lollipop stick** by trimming a toothpick to the desired length. Insert the sharp end into the coil; if you want to hang your charm, insert an eye pin into the end opposite from the stick.

3. **Bake according to the directions** on the polymer clay package. Allow to cool. Coat with clear nail polish and allow to dry. After baking, you can remove the eye pin, dip it in strong bonding glue, and reinsert it.

Chocolate

1 Flatten balls of brown clay into pancakes and then wrap each around different-colored balls of clay. Roll with your hands to smooth out the surface. Lightly press to flatten the bottoms of each ball.

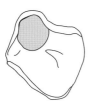

wrap

2 Make "frosting" decorations by rolling leftover clay into thin logs and pressing them onto the surface of each chocolate in decorative patterns. If you want to hang your charm, insert an eye pin into the top of the chocolate before baking.

decorate

3 Bake according to the directions on the polymer clay package. Allow to cool. Coat with clear nail polish and allow to dry. Note that, after baking, you can remove the eye pin, dip it in strong bonding glue, and reinsert it.

Secured into the baked clay with bonding glue, metal eye pins make it easy to loop your charms onto necklaces, ribbons, keychains—whatever you like.

Nobody wants lumpy chocolates! Trim excess clay from the outer layer before completely wrapping it around the ball.

For an even more lifelike look, you can use a pen cap to take mini "bites" out of clay treats before baking. Any of these charms can be attached to a ring blank—see Ideas for Modifying Microcrafts (page 84) for a simple how-to!

Actual size: About ¾ inch tall
Designed by: Mel Sparkles

CATS

The perfect present for fans of our furry friends, these little felt kitties are so easy and fun to make. They fit snugly into envelopes or boxes and enjoy hanging around your cubbies and cupboards.

SUPPLIES

tracing paper

disappearing fabric marker

scissors

felt scraps

yarn scraps

embroidery thread and needle

craft paints

toothpick *or* small paintbrush

1 **Trace the body pattern** onto tracing paper and cut out the shape. Then trace the pattern twice (for the front and back) onto the felt.

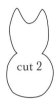

cut 2

2 **Cut out the felt pieces** along the inside of the marked lines. Place the 2 pieces together.

3 **Make the tail** by inserting a small scrap of yarn between the pieces of felt. Starting at the tail, use tiny stitches to sew around the edge of the body. Leave a small opening for stuffing.

4 **Gently stuff the body** with scraps of yarn. Sew the opening closed.

5 **Paint on a face and markings.** Dipping the end of a toothpick in paint and gently pressing it against the felt is a great way to add eyes and noses. Whiskers and stripes are easily made using the same technique. (A small paintbrush works, too.)

Nail-art paintbrushes found at the beauty supply store work nicely for painting details onto miniature critters.

Have fun creating different kitty breeds. A Siamese can be made by painting a black muzzle and ears onto a white body. Channel your inner tiger by painting black stripes on an orange body. Or add spots to make a fierce little leopard or cheetah. Rawr!

Actual size: About 2 inches tall
Designed by: Katie Hatz

DEER HEADS

No miniature deer were harmed in the making of this project! Spruce up any corner of your house with a little woodsy decor. The best part is, this quick and simple sculpture requires nothing but a ball of clay, a scrap of cardboard, and a couple twigs.

SUPPLIES

tracing paper

⅛-inch-thick cardboard *or* illustration board

craft knife

craft glue

paint *or* spray paint

1-inch ball of polymer or modeling clay,
 plus a bit more for ears

ruler

clay tools or toothpick

twigs

magnet, tack, *or* hook-and-loop tape (for hanging)

1 **Trace the plaque patterns** onto tracing paper and cut out the shapes. Then trace each shape onto the cardboard and cut out. Glue the smaller piece on top of the larger one. Paint it whatever color you'd like and allow it to dry.

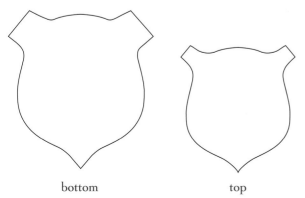

bottom   top

2 **Roll the clay ball** between your palms until it's about 2 inches long and tapered at one end. Form it into an S, with one end a little fatter than the other. Flatten the bigger end against a table or other surface—this is where the deer's neck will attach to the plaque. Sculpt the smaller end into a simple deer-head shape.

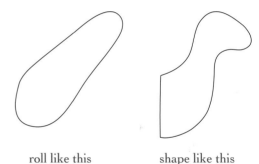

roll like this   shape like this

3 **Make the ears** by forming the leftover clay into 2 ¼-inch blobs. Flatten each blob into an oval and pinch the end until it resembles an ear. Press the ears onto the head and gently smooth out the seam with your hands. Use clay tools or a toothpick to get into the small spaces and make sure the ears are securely attached.

4 **Make room for the antlers.** Use a clay tool or toothpick to press 2 holes (large enough to fit the twigs) about ⅛ to ¼ inch deep into the top of the head.

5 **Bake according to the directions** on the polymer clay package. Allow to cool. Then paint the head, if desired.

6 **Glue the head to the plaque** first and then glue the twig antlers into the holes. Affix a magnet, tack, or hook-and-loop tape to the back of the plaque. Now you're ready to hang your diminutive deer wherever you need a little cheer.

More Microtaxidermy

Why stop at just a deer head? Use leftover clay and cardboard to create your very own mini menagerie!

SUPPLIES

polymer or modeling clay

clay tools *or* toothpick

1/8-inch-thick cardboard *or* illustration board

craft knife

craft glue

paint

googly eyes (optional)

twistable wire (optional)

1 **Choose one or more animals** to keep your mini deer company. Use our list below, or come up with your own. You can even invent animals if you want! Some ideas to get you started:

Bear	Giraffe
Fish	Squirrel
Pheasant	Chicken
Lion	Jackalope
Hedgehog	Owl
Goat	Zebra
Octopus	Dinosaur
Wolf	Fox
Armadillo	Kitten

2 **Using a photograph as reference,** create your animal out of modeling clay. You may even want to find photos depicting multiple angles of your animal. Be as realistic or as creative as you want—exaggerating your animal's proprotions can give it even more personality.

3 **Bake according to the directions** on the polymer clay package. Allow to cool. (Note: If your animal is larger, hollowing out a cavity before you put it in the oven will ensure quick and even baking.)

4 **Place your animal on a piece of cardboard** and sketch an appropriately sized shape for its plaque. You can adapt the shape on the previous page, or come up with your own. Rectangles and ovals always work in a pinch.

5 **Assemble and paint the plaque** and allow to dry. Glue your animal to the plaque, holding it steady until it's dry enough to stay put on its own.

6 **Repeat** as many times as necessary to create a delightful woodland (or farm or jungle) scene!

Jazz up your mini animals with mini eyeballs! Use tweezers or needlenose pliers to carefully place googly eyes where you want them.

Use your imagination to set up different scenarios with your taxidermied mini kingdom. Are your animals friends or foes—or even stars of their own nature show?

Actual size: Varies
Designed by: Holly Keller

DOGS

Save felt scraps to sew a little-bitty bowwow. And why stop at that?
You can make your puppy a bandanna collar, a cozy bed, some bones, a dish,
and his very own dog toys. Rrruff!

SUPPLIES

tracing paper

disappearing fabric marker *or* sharp black pencil

scissors

1 8-x-8-in piece of felt

1 patterned cotton fabric scrap

scraps of felt for eye patch and muzzle

1 scrap of red *or* pink felt for tongue

pins

sewing machine *or* needle and thread

polyester fiberfill for stuffing

bamboo skewer *or* stuffing tool

black embroidery thread and needle

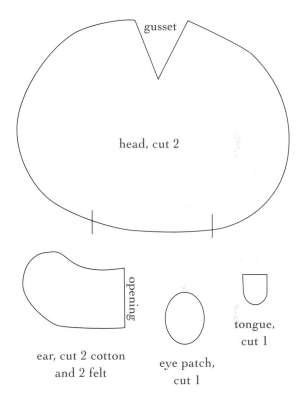

gusset

head, cut 2

opening

ear, cut 2 cotton
and 2 felt

eye patch,
cut 1

tongue,
cut 1

1. **Trace the dog patterns** onto the tracing paper and cut out. Then trace the patterns onto the felt, leaving at least ½ inch of space around your traced edges. Cut out the felt pieces, leaving about ¼ inch of fabric around the lines for the seam allowance.

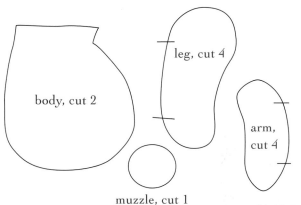

leg, cut 4

body, cut 2

arm,
cut 4

muzzle, cut 1

2. **Pin and sew** together the patterned cotton to the felt ear pieces, right sides together. Turn out. Sew together the patterned cotton and felt ear pieces, sewing along traced lines, leaving ears open at top. Trim excess fabric around the edge of your seam, leaving a ¼- to ⅛-inch edge. Turn out, gently pushing out the edges. Now top-stitch around the edge of the ears so your stitches show on the patterned-fabric side of the ears.

3. **Sew the gusset closed** on both head pieces. Pin the ears in place, with the raw edges along the top of the head and the brown felt facing out. Pin the head pieces together, right sides together. With the gusset seams on each piece aligned at the top, sew around the edge, catching the ears in the seam. Leave an opening as indicated on the pattern and turn right-side out.

4   **Firmly stuff the head.** Turn in the raw edges and close with an invisible ladder stitch (for how, see page 83).

5   **Pin the two body pieces together** and sew along traced lines, leaving the neck open. Trim excess fabric (as you did with the ears) and turn out. Repeat this process with the arms and legs. Use a bamboo skewer or other pointed stuffing tool to turn out these small parts.

6   **Firmly stuff the body** and then sew a long running stitch around the neck; cinch it closed, turning in the raw edges. Stuff the leg and arm pieces, turn in the raw edges, and, using a small ladder stitch, sew the openings closed on each piece.

7   **Attach the head** to the neck using a whipstitch.

8   **Attach the legs** to the body using a small diagonal stitch at the top of one leg; then push the needle through the entire body to the other side and repeat with the other leg. Push the needle back through the body and make another small diagonal stitch across the first a few times to make an *X*. This method of attachment makes the legs movable. Repeat to attach the arms.

9   **Hand stitch scraps of felt** onto the head to make patches as desired. Using the black embroidery thread, embroider a belly button with a small *X*, use a satin stitch to embroider eyes and a nose, and use a split stitch to embroider a mouth. You may wish first to draw the facial features on the dog's face with a disappearing fabric marker.

10   **To make a bandanna collar,** cut 2 scraps of patterned cotton fabric into an oblong triangle long enough to wrap around your dog's neck. Pin the scraps together, right sides facing together. Sew along the lines, leaving an opening, then turn out though the opening, and iron. Fold in the raw edges and topstitch around the edge of the entire bandanna, closing the opening in the process.

This handsome bandanna collar is removable, so your pup can wear a different one each season.

Set your sewing machine to use a smaller stitch, or use extra-small hand stitches, when sewing tiny pieces. See page 83 for tips on tiny sewing techniques.

Little Dog Accessories

Not the most experienced seamster or seamstress? This little toy dog is just as adorable as its pal — and makes a perfect simple project for beginners. Then make a ball, bowl and bones, and a cozy dog bed.

SUPPLIES

scraps of white and brown felt for toy

scraps of felt in 3 colors for ball

1 piece of red felt for bowl, 2 by 5 in

1 piece of white felt for bones, 1 ½ by 4 in

1 piece of patterned cotton fabric for dog bed sides, 3 by 8 ½ in

1 piece of contrasting cotton fabric for dog bed base, 5 by 5 in

1 mini button for dog bed

Toy

1 **Trace the toy patterns** onto the tracing paper and cut out. Then trace the body pattern onto the scrap of white felt twice (front and back) and the gusset pattern on the white felt once. Trace the ear pattern on the scrap of brown felt twice. Cut out the shapes.

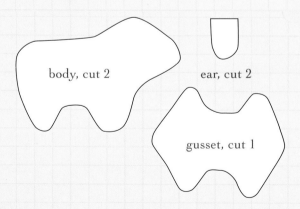

body, cut 2

ear, cut 2

gusset, cut 1

2 **Sew 1 body piece** to the gusset piece using a tiny whipstitch along their aligned edges. Your stitches will remain exposed on this piece, so take care when hand sewing. Repeat to attach the other body piece to the other edge of the gusset. Hand sew together the top edges of the body, leaving a small opening at the rear of the dog for stuffing.

3 **Gently stuff the dog,** using a bamboo skewer or other pointed stuffing tool to reach into the head and legs. Whipstitch the opening closed; hand sew the ears to the head.

4 **Cut out 1 tiny circle** of brown felt to make the mouth and 2 tiny ovals of felt for spots. Whipstitch these pieces onto the dog as desired. Separate 2 strands of black embroidery thread and embroider the face on the dog using 2 French knots for the eyes, a small row of satin stitches for the nose, and an upside-down Y for the mouth.

Ball

1 **Trace the ball pattern** onto the tracing paper and cut out; then trace the pattern on the felt twice for each color. Cut out 6 shapes total.

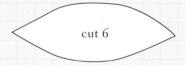

cut 6

2 **Sew together** 2 different-colored felt pieces along a long edge. Repeat with another 2 felt pieces. Then sew another felt piece to each pair and then, right sides together, sew the 2 pieces of the ball together, leaving an opening for stuffing.

3 **Turn out and stuff firmly.** Turn in the raw edges and sew the opening closed using an invisible ladder stitch.

4 **Cut out 2 tiny circles** from a remaining scrap of felt. Sew the circles to the top and bottom of the ball to make a pretty finish that covers any gaps or flaws in alignment.

Bowl and Bones

1 **Trace the bowl and bones patterns** onto the tracing paper and cut out. Then trace the bowl patterns onto the red felt and the bone patterns onto the white felt. Cut out the shapes.

2 **Whipstitch one long edge** of the bowl sides around the circumference of the bottom of your bowl base, aligning the raw edges. Sew together the short edges of the bowl sides to close the bowl bottom. Trim excess length. Fold the bowl sides up underneath so the folded edge is at the top of the bowl; this makes the bowl shorter and sturdier.

3 **Fold each bone piece** in half and pin in place. Top-stitch along the unfolded edge of each to keep them folded. Knot the felt at both ends to make each bone about 1 inch long, trimming any excess felt.

Bed

1 **Trace the bed patterns** onto the tracing paper and cut out the shapes. Fold the fabric for the sides of the bed in half lengthwise. Pin the traced sides to the fabric, aligning with the fold, and cut out the shape. Pin the base to the remaining piece of fabric and cut out 2.

2 **Pin and sew together** the folded fabric for the sides, rights sides facing, and the 2 base pieces, as indicated on the pattern. Turn out and stuff very lightly. (The sides should remain mostly flat after stuffing.) Turn in the raw edges and use an invisible ladder stitch to close the openings.

3 **Sew the mini button** to the center of the base. Sew the sides to the base using a small whipstitch along the circumference of the lower edge of the base.

Keep your bed pattern this size to keep a toy dog (like the fellow on page 29) snuggly, or scan and resize it 200% to fit the bigger puppy on page 24.

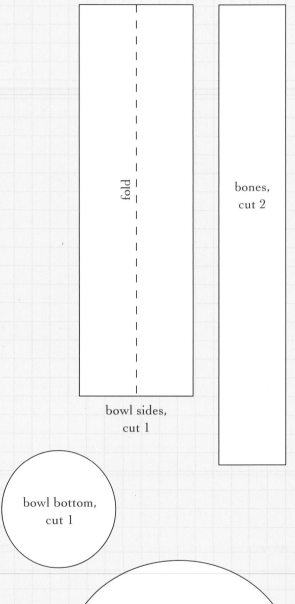

fold

bones, cut 2

bowl sides, cut 1

bowl bottom, cut 1

bed base, cut 2

bed sides, cut 1

It's a dog-eat-dog world.

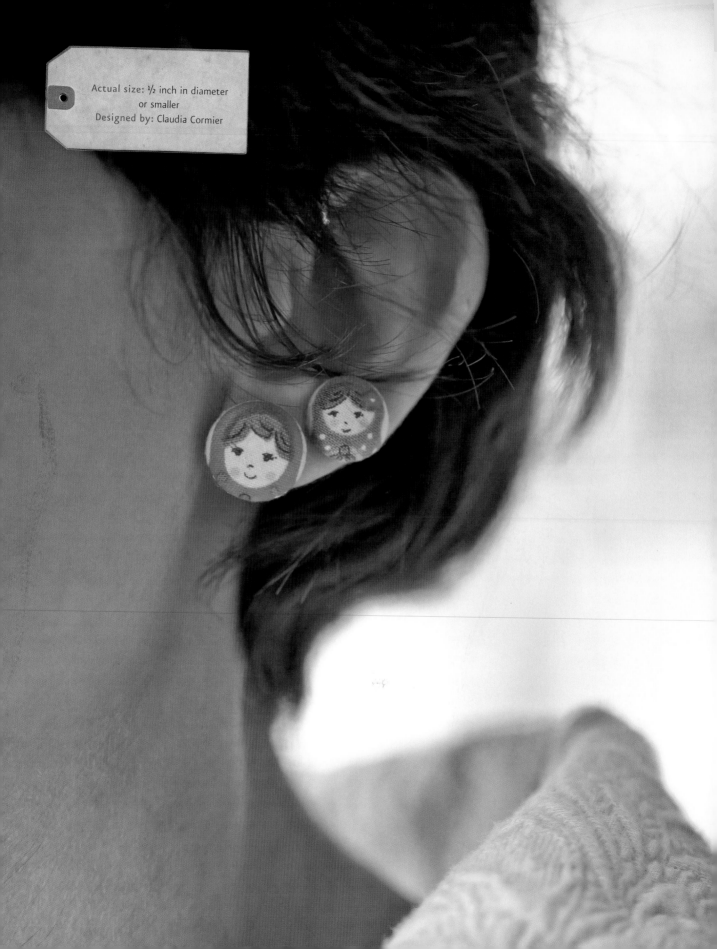

Actual size: ½ inch in diameter
or smaller
Designed by: Claudia Cormier

FABRIC BUTTONS

Have you ever stared at a fabric pattern and fallen in love with one of the details? With a basic button cover kit, you can turn a little piece of a pretty print into earrings, brooches, or buttons. This kind of jewelrymaking is easy-peasy.

SUPPLIES

button cover kit, size 30 or smaller

1-in-square piece of cardboard (such as a
 scrap from the kit box)

disappearing fabric marker

scissors

5-in-square piece of lightweight fabric

craft glue

2 post-style earring blanks and backs

1. **Trace the button** from the kit onto the cardboard and neatly cut out the circle. This makes a template "window" that you can place over your fabric to see what the finished design will look like.

frame your pattern

2. **Trace a circle** onto 2 identical pieces of fabric, using the cardboard template. Cut out the shapes.

3. **Place the fabric**, right side down, inside the plastic shell from the kit. Place the button blank inside the shell over the fabric. Fold the excess fabric inside the blank and adjust the fabric to make sure that it's centered. Place the flat back on top of the folded fabric and push with the metal tool until you hear a "pop." Repeat with the remaining piece of fabric to make a matching earring.

4. **Glue the post-style blanks** to the flat side of the buttons. Set aside to dry.

If you need to remove the button to recenter it, just turn it upside down and push it out with your fingers.

You can purchase a kit with flat backs or remove the shanks with pliers so it's easy to attach earring backs.

Actual size: 2 inches tall
Designed by: Larissa Holland

FLOWER POCKET
PENDANTS

Blossoms cut from scraps of felt are a lovely way to hide a secret pocket pendant.
Enclose a tiny note or a photo to carry with you wherever you go.

SUPPLIES

wool or wool-felt blend scraps in assorted colors

1 8½-by-11-in piece of freezer paper

1 8½-by-11-in piece of office paper

inkjet printer

scissors

iron

fabric glue

toothpick

tweezers (optional)

needle and embroidery thread in contrasting colors

pencil

1 scrap of quilter's plastic or cardboard

⅛-in-wide scrap ribbon

needle and invisible thread

chain or ribbon necklace

1 **Plan the colors** for your pendant, leaves, and flowers before tracing and cutting the pieces (see pattern on page 34).

2 **Mark a small *X*** in the corner of the nonshiny side of the freezer paper for your reference. Using an iron on medium heat, adhere the freezer paper, shiny side down, onto the office paper. Keep the iron moving and make sure the edges are sealed. Use this paper "sandwich" to print the pattern template at 100 percent on your inkjet printer. Be

sure the pattern prints on the freezer-paper side (where your *X* marks the spot!). Peel the freezer paper from the office paper.

3 **Rough cut the pattern pieces,** cutting around (but not on) the lines. Carefully cut the pendant interior piece on the lines.

4 **Using an iron on medium heat,** adhere the freezer-paper pattern pieces to the appropriate felt scraps. Hold the tip of the iron very briefly, just so the freezer paper adheres lightly to the felt. Cut out the felt pieces along the lines. Peel off the freezer-paper pattern only as you use each piece, so you can keep track of which is which.

5 **Tack down the pocket** to the back, flush with the bottom and sides, by using a toothpick to apply tiny dabs of fabric glue to the outside edges.

6 **Hold each flower circle** with your fingers or tweezers and cut small slits and wedges to create the look of flower petals.

cutting guide for flowers

1
slits at N, S,
E, and W

2
wedge from
right of slits

3
completed
wedges

4
for #2
flower only,
additional
tiny wedges
(optional)

7 **Stack each small flower circle** onto a larger flower by applying a tiny dot of fabric glue with a toothpick. Glue on leaves and flowers using this diagram as a reference.

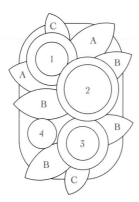

placement guide

8 **Embroider the leaves and flowers** (as shown in the photo) using a backstitch and French knots. Leave space around the edges so the stitches won't show on the sides of the pendant. Embroider separately the leaves that overlap the edges of the pendant. Be sure not to pull too tightly as you sew because tight stitches may cause the pendant front to curl or lose its shape. Decorate any bare areas of the pendant using French knots, if desired.

9 **Trace the pendant interior pattern** onto the quilter's plastic and cut out. Glue it to the back of the front piece.

10 **Add a loop** by folding the ribbon to an appropriate length and glue the raw ends together. Then glue the ribbon loop to the top of the plastic, overlapping the pendant about ¼ inch. Glue the halves of the pendant together, aligning the edges and making sure the pocket opens toward the ribbon loop.

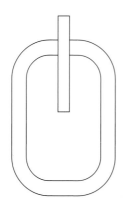

placement of ribbon loop
and plastic interior piece on
back of pendant front

11 **Backstitch around the entire pendant,** a fat ⅟₁₆ inch from the edges using invisible thread, reinforcing the stitches at the ribbon loop. (See page 83 for stitches.) Carefully lift the leaves and petals and sew underneath them as you go. String the pendant onto your favorite chain or ribbon.

backstitching shown from back and front

Tuck photos or little notes inside your pocket pendants.

Flower Pocket Pendant
Pattern Pieces

Tracing tiny patterns by hand can be tedious. Here's a handy trick: print on fortified freezer paper. Visit quirkbooks.com/microcrafts to download these patterns, and print according to the instructions on page 33.

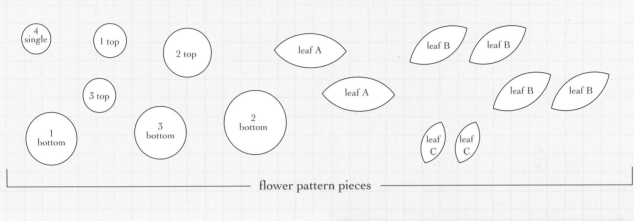

4 single

1 top

2 top

leaf A

leaf B

leaf B

3 top

leaf A

leaf B

leaf B

1 bottom

3 bottom

2 bottom

leaf C

leaf C

— flower pattern pieces —

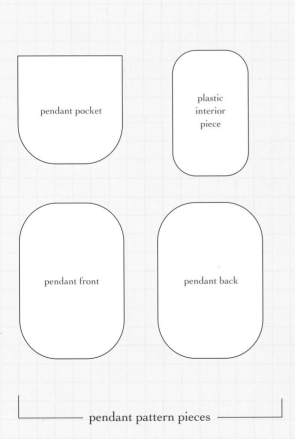

pendant pocket

plastic interior piece

pendant front

pendant back

— pendant pattern pieces —

Some of the pattern pieces are super small and hard to pick up with your fingers. Use the sharp end of your craft knife to pick up and place them accurately.

Actual size: 2 inches tall
Designed by: Larissa Holland

GREETING CARDS

Here's a nice little way to say, "Hello." Trace or print out these fairy-tale patterns for delicate cut-paper cards and micro-envelopes. Vary the designs to make your own holiday greetings, birthday cards, pop-ups, or valentines, as simple or as intricate as you like.

SUPPLIES

card stock scraps in assorted colors

colored gel pens and pencils (optional)

tracing paper

scissors

pencil

inkjet printer

craft knife and cutting mat

1 8½-by-11-in piece of prepared freezer paper

1 8½-by-11-in piece of office paper

iron

ruler

gel glue for paper

toothpick

¼-in-round pop dots (or foam dots), ¹⁄₁₆-inch thick

¼-in hole punch

⅛-in hole punch

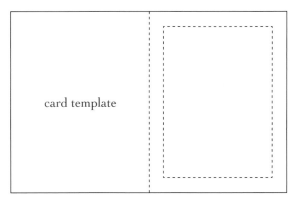

card template

1 **Plan the colors for your card.** Use patterned card stock or draw tiny designs and stripes onto the card stock using gel pens and sharp colored pencils, if desired.

2 **Trace the card template** onto the tracing paper (or visit quirkbooks.com/microcrafts for a free download to print) and cut out the shape. Then trace the template onto card stock. Using a ruler to guide your craft knife, carefully cut out the shape. Using the blade's dull side, score the card down the center, but don't fold it just yet.

3 **Mark a small *X*** on a corner of the nonshiny side of your freezer paper. Using an iron on medium heat, adhere the freezer paper, shiny side down, onto the office paper. Keep the iron moving and make sure the edges are sealed. Use this paper "sandwich" to print the pattern template at 100 percent through your inkjet printer. Be sure the pattern prints on the freezer-paper side (where your *X* marks the spot!). Peel the freezer paper from the office paper.

4 **Rough cut all the pattern pieces,** cutting around but not on the lines. Using an iron on medium heat, adhere the freezer-paper pattern pieces to the card stock. Cut out the pieces along the lines. Peel off the freezer paper.

5 **Assemble your card,** starting with the background rectangle and adding pieces according to the diagrams (pages 38 to 40). To attach the pieces, dab a small amount of gel glue onto a scrap piece of card stock and use a toothpick to apply it sparingly.

6 **Attach your assembled design to the card front** by applying glue with a toothpick inside the rectangular guideline. Allow it to dry. Fold the card in half. The inside is blank for your handwritten message.

Little Red Riding Hood Card

hood

napkin

cape

tree 3

tree 1

dress

cloud

cloud top

basket

background

tree 2 middle

tree 2 top

tree 2 bottom

tree 2 base

Red Riding Hood pattern, cut 1 of each

finished card, enlarged to show detail

1 **First, build up the forest background.**

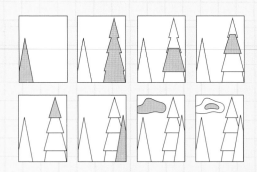

2 **Then put Red together.**

¼-in hole punch, cut in half, with tiny notch for bangs

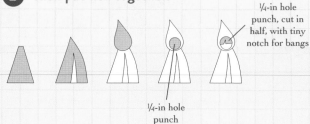

¼-in hole punch

3 **Put her in the forest and add the finishing touches.**

pop dot

⅛-in hole punch

Gel glue is forgiving, so you'll have a few moments to finesse each piece before it sets.

Hansel and Gretel Card

finished card, enlarged to show detail

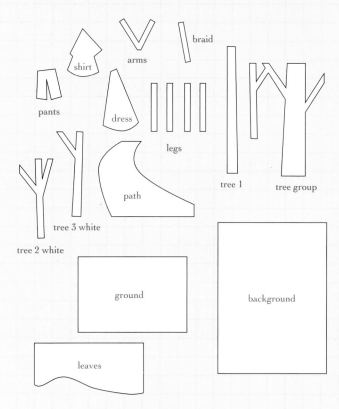

shirt

arms

braid

pants

dress

legs

tree 1

tree group

tree 3 white

path

tree 2 white

ground

background

leaves

Hansel and Gretel pattern, cut 1 of each

1 Layer the background on the card.

Cut a ¼-inch pop dot in half, and put one half under each figure.

2 Make Hansel and Gretel.

¼-in hole punch

¼-in hole punch

⅛-in hole punches

3 Add the finishing touches.

Cut a very thin strip of ivory card stock into tiny squares for bread crumbs.

✕ ✕ ✕ 39 ✕ ✕ ✕

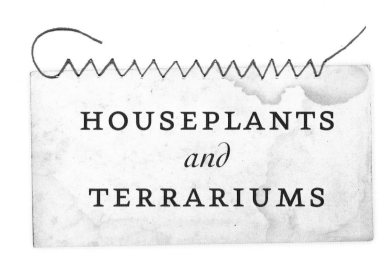

HOUSEPLANTS *and* TERRARIUMS

Whether you live in a big country house or a teeny city apartment, it's easy to tend a wee secret garden. Any small container will do: Mini terra cotta pots are available at garden centers and craft stores, but household items like teacups, shot glasses, and thimbles can add a dash of whimsical charm.

SUPPLIES

any little container *or* jar with lid

handful of potting mix or garden soil

miniature plants or cuttings

hammer and nail *or* wire mesh (for terrarium)

1 **Fill the container** with dirt and gently pat it down. Use your pinky finger to make an indentation about ⅓-inch deep. Place your plant or cutting in the hole and pat down the soil to fill.

2 **Water gently.** Just be careful not to flood the little pot! It's fun to use an eye dropper, plant mister, or dollhouse watering can, which will also help prevent overwatering. Small pots dry out quickly, so water as needed.

3 **Provide adequate light,** depending on the type of plant you choose.

4 **To make a terrarium,** punch holes in a jar lid with a hammer and nail, or cut a bit of wire mesh to fit the top of the jar. Place your container or terrarium in a macramé hanger (see page 44) and hang it from a windowsill.

Adding a bottom layer of pebbles and/or activated charcoal can help with drainage.

Cuttings from spider plants, jade, and string of pearls thrive in small containers. Bonsais, mini ferns, dwarf mosses, and micro-orchids are available at greenhouses and online.

Macramé Hanger

Make your houseplant mobile! This fun and retro plant holder is easy to whip up and is perfect for hanging your little pot in a window or even from your earlobe. (See "Ideas for Modifying Microcrafts," page 84, for a jewelrymaking how-to.)

SUPPLIES

8 yards of thin cord *or* embroidery thread *or* string
¼-inch jump ring

1 **Cut 8 lengths of cord,** each 36 inches long, and two lengths of cord, each 18 inches long. Use one 18-inch piece to completely cover the jump ring with half hitch knots. Fold the 36-inch pieces over and through the covered ring. Use the remaining piece of cord to tie a ¼-inch wrap knot around all the cords to gather them at the base of the jump ring. Hide the ends of the knot.

half hitch knot   wrap knot

2 **Tie ¼ inch of half-knot twists** on each group of four cords. To create a half-knot twist, tie one-half of a square knot (as shown below), and repeat multiple times beginning with the left piece of cord.

half-knot twist

3 **Drop down ¼ inch** and tie a row of alternating square knots to connect the left two cords in each group with the right two of the group next to it. (To make a square knot, do steps 1 and 2 above, and then repeat, starting with the right cord this time.) Repeat this step two more times.

 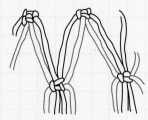

square knot   alternating square knots

4 **Place your chosen container** into the hanger to make sure it will fit, and then tie a ¼-inch wrap knot. Cut off and fray the ends as desired.

Knotted cord, thread, or string makes for mini macramé.

Wire Plant Stand

Twist thick wire to make a little stand. Use needlenose pliers
and wire cutters to bend and cut.

SUPPLIES

2 yards thick florist's wire in your choice of colors
needlenose pliers
wire cutters

1 **Cut the wire** into four equal lengths. Bend a curved foot into the end of each piece of wire, using the pliers to create a tight spiral.

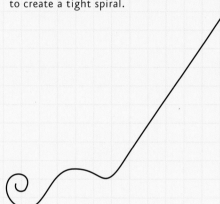

make decorative feet

2 **Hold all 4 pieces of wire together,** right where they begin to curve outward. Begin to twist the pieces with each other, keeping them evenly fanned out to produce a regular twisting pattern. Continue until you have about 3 inches of twisted wire.

3 **Bend 2 pieces** of wire off to one side and continue twisting them for another 2 inches. Bend into a large curve with a little hook at the end and cut off the excess wire.

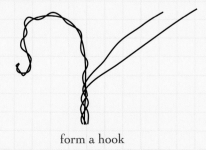

form a hook

4 **Twist the remaining 2 pieces** all the way to their ends and bend into a second, higher hook. Trim to desired length.

5 **Bend the feet at 90-degree angles** and place on a level surface. Adjust as needed to make your stand sturdy and symmetrical. Hang your favorite microplants on the hooks for balance and display with pride!

This handy stand is also great for holding your favorite earrings. But beware of microdinosaurs that can climb!

Actual size: ½ to 1 inch long
Designed by: Mel Sparkles

LADYBUGS, BUMBLEBEES, *and* BUTTERFLIES

Bzzz! Who knew bugs could be so charming? You can make these little insects into jewelry, pin them to greeting cards, or tuck them into Flower Pocket Pendants (see page 33) for a whimsical touch.

SUPPLIES

tracing paper

disappearing fabric marker

felt scrap

scissors

lace scraps (for bee and butterfly)

sewing thread and needle

yarn *or* fabric scraps, for stuffing

craft paints

toothpick *or* small paintbrush

1 **Trace your chosen pattern** onto the tracing paper and cut out the shape. Then use a marker to trace the pattern twice onto the felt (for the front and back). Cut out the shapes.

bee and ladybug, cut 2 for each one

butterfly, cut 2

2 **Make the bug's body** by placing the 2 felt pieces together. To make wings for a bee or butterfly, insert 2 scraps of lace between the felt pieces. Pinch the pieces together while you sew tiny stitches around the edge. Leave a small opening for stuffing.

3 **Gently stuff your bug** with yarn or fabric scraps. If necessary, use a pointed object to help pack the stuffing (a bamboo skewer or crochet hook works well). Stitch the opening closed and knot the thread to secure.

4 **Bring your bug to life** by painting a face, spots, stripes, or other markings using craft paints and a toothpick or small paintbrush.

Watered-down paint (or watercolors) can be used to add subtle color to butterfly wings. Sequins can also be added for an extra bit of magic. Try tiny rhinestones to make sparkly ladybug spots.

Actual size: Smaller than a
matchbox
Designed by: Holly Keller

MONSTER BABIES

Monster babies are too cute to be scary. Customize their expressions with a varied number of eyes, teeth, and stitch marks.

SUPPLIES

tracing paper

pencil

3-in-square piece of felt

scrap of white felt

hole punch

pins

needle *and* embroidery thread in black, white, *and* a color that matches your monster

craft glue

polyester fiberfill for stuffing

disappearing fabric marker

small paintbrush *or* toothpick

You don't want your monsters to lose their stuffing. See page 83 for tiny stitching techniques.

1 **Trace the body pattern** onto the tracing paper and cut out. Then trace the pattern twice onto the felt. Cut out the shapes. Punch out 1 or 2 (or even 3!) circles from the white felt using the hole punch to make as many eyeballs for your monster as you like.

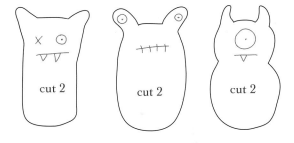

2 **Glue on the punched felt** for eye(s) and let dry. Use black embroidery thread to stitch a French knot into the center of each eye; embroider the remaining features, using a split stitch for the mouth and a satin stitch for the teeth. It's easy to stitch a belly button with an *X*.

3 **Pin together the body pieces,** wrong sides facing. Double thread the embroidery needle and use a blanket stitch to sew the pieces together, leaving a small opening at the bottom. (See page 83 for stitching instructions.) Insert just enough stuffing to make your little monster three-dimensional and then use a blanket stitch to close.

Monster Babies' Accessories

If you make little diapers and matchbox beds, your monsters will have nothing to be grumpy about!

SUPPLIES

tracing paper
pencil
scrap of white felt
pins
needle *and* embroidery thread
matchbox
scraps of colorful fabric
craft glue

Diaper

1 **Trace the diaper pattern** onto the tracing paper and cut it out. Then trace the pattern onto the white felt and cut it out.

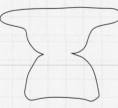

diaper, cut 1

2 **Fold the diaper piece** to align the top and bottom (except the tabs on the bottom half) and fold the tabs around the front of the diaper. Pin and stitch in place.

3 **Slip the diaper onto the monster** so that he doesn't get fussy.

Matchbox Bed

1 **Glue 1 piece of fabric** to the interior of a matchbox and another around the outside, or paint like on page 68.

2 **Cut another piece of fabric** for a sheet, and fray the edges about ¼ inch all around, as shown below.

Use a sewing needle or pin to work individual threads loose and create a pretty fringed finish.

In winter, take pity on chilly monsters and knit warm matchbox-bed blankies. See page 70 for a how-to.

A cross stitch makes a cute innie belly button. Or use a French knot (page 83) to make an outie.

Actual size: 1 ½ by 2 inches
Designed by: Sarah Goldschadt

OWLS

Don't let pretty scraps of fabric go to waste.
Dainty owlies can be made out of any 3-inch cotton square.

SUPPLIES

tracing paper

disappearing fabric marker

2 3-in-square scraps of fabric (one print and
  one solid)

scissors

sewing machine *or* needle *and* thread

bamboo skewer (optional)

embroidery thread *and* needle

polyester fiberfill

2 **Cut out the fabric pieces.** With right sides facing, sew together the fabric pieces using a ⅛-inch seam allowance. Leave the opening unsewn as marked on the pattern. Turn right-side out through the opening; use a pointed object like a bamboo skewer to push out the corners.

3 **Make the beak** by folding down the triangle. Use 2 straight stitches of embroidery thread to secure it to the front, sewing through the tip of the triangle and 1 layer of the body fabric. Knot the thread on the inside of the beak.

4 **Mark spots for the eyes** using the fabric marker. Use embroidery thread and small straight stitches to make the eyes; knot the thread on the inside.

5 **Stuff the body** and fold in the bottom edge. Double-thread a needle and sew a running stitch along the bottom. Gather the ends and secure with a knot.

1 **Trace the owl pattern** onto tracing paper and cut out the shape. Then trace the pattern twice onto the wrong side of the fabric (for the front and back).

cut 2

leave an opening

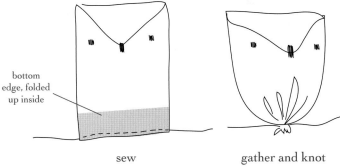

bottom edge, folded up inside

sew

gather and knot

Sew on a loop of matching embroidery thread to make owls into ornaments you can hang around the house or tie onto gift packages.

Actual size: 1½ by 2 inches
Designed by: Nadia Marks Wojcik

PARTY HATS

Who doesn't love a cute and snappy chapeau? Whip up these simple hats to keep your special friends forever festive.

SUPPLIES

scrap paper
bamboo skewer
pom-poms
craft glue

1. **Trace the pattern** onto tracing paper and cut out the shape. Then trace the pattern onto the paper scraps and cut out the shapes. Roll each shape into a cone, overlapping the edges about ¼ inch. A small gap should be at the top of the cone. Glue and allow to dry.

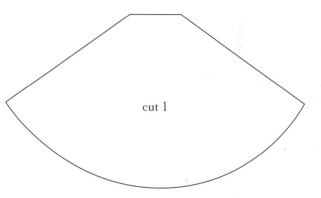

cut 1

2. **Trim the pointed end** of a bamboo skewer to 4 inches. Poke this end through the small gap at the top of the cone, from bottom to top.

3. **Apply a pom-pom** with a drop of glue.

Decorate party hats for little snowmen—or use them as cupcake toppers instead.

Paper Balloons

Need an impromptu party favor or gift? Cut balloons out of thick, colorful paper and attach them to bendable floral wire or toothpicks.

SUPPLIES

tracing paper

pencil

scraps of card stock *or* thick paper

markers *or* a printer

scissors

tape *or* glue

7-in piece of white wrapped floral wire

Customize your balloons by writing mini messages or drawing silly faces or pictures on them!

1 **Trace the balloon pattern** onto tracing paper and cut out the shape. Trace the pattern on card stock as many times as desired. Cut out the shapes.

2 **Glue a piece of wire** to the back of each balloon and set aside to dry.

3 **Arrange the balloons in staggering heights.** Hold the wires together about 1½ inches below the lowest balloon and twist the bottoms of the wires together.

Floral wire makes a great base for twisting ballons around and into stuff: miniature bear friends (page 22), house-plants, cakes, you name it.

Actual size: ½ to 3 in
Designed by: Alicia Kachmar
and Melaine Kachmar

PLANETS

Pluto's been kicked out of the solar system? Not in our book!
Pay homage to the little blue (ex-)planet and its eight cosmic buddies
with these easy balls of felted fluff.

SUPPLIES

scraps of bulky-weight wool yarn in varied colors

hand soap

paper towels

2 long match sticks, dowel rods, *or* BBQ skewers

fishing line

glue

1. **Start by separating strands of yarn** for each planet so that you have a fuzz-ball clump. You'll need 20 to 40 inches of yarn per planet, depending on the size of the planet and the weight of the yarn.

untwist plies

pull fibers apart

2. **Wet a clump of yarn** under hot—but not scalding—running water. Add hand soap to the clump and start rolling it into a ball under the running water. It should form a ball within about a minute. Repeat with the remaining 8 clumps of yarn.

3. **Set aside each clump** on a paper towel to dry completely. It may take about a day.

4. **To make a mobile,** cut the heads off 2 long match sticks or use dowel rods, BBQ skewers, or tree branches cut to length. Position like an *X* and wrap string or fishing line around the middle, knotting at the beginning and end and securing with glue.

5. **Cut 9 strands of fishing line** for hanging planets, but make each one twice the length you want. Thread a needle with fishing line and feed through planet until half is on each side. Then thread the other end of fishing line back through bottom of the planet so that both ends are coming out from the top. Tie a knot around the top of each planet with one end of the fishing line, snip and tuck it inside the planet. Tie the other end around part of the mobile, and secure with glue. Repeat with the rest of the planets.

Hot, soapy water transforms yarn scraps into felt, in a snap!

The sky's the limit! You can hang stars made of sparkly yarn or even toy spaceships from your mobile.

Actual size: 1 to 2 inches
Designed by: Elizabeth Duke

PORCUPINE *and* FRIENDS

It's quilling time! This fun and easy microcraft, popularized in the '90s, is the arrangement of skinny strips of paper coiled, bent, or pinched into any shape or design you like—from flowers to porcupines to kites. These 3-D delights can be used to adorn greeting cards, box tops, or any other flat surface.

SUPPLIES

⅛-in-wide quilling paper in assorted colors
slotted quilling needle *or* tapestry needle with
 a big eye
craft glue
wax paper
pins (optional)

To make quilled flowers, glue teardrop shapes together.

1 **Make a circle for the porcupine body** by wrapping 18 inches of paper around the needle in a tight spiral. Glue down the end and allow to dry. Pull the middle of the circle to one side, secure with a pin if desired, and glue. When dry, pinch one side into a sharp tip to make a teardrop shape.

2 **Make a teardrop for the head** by wrapping 8 inches of paper around the needle. Glue down the end. When dry, pinch one side into a sharp tip.

3 **Make the feet** by forming 2 loose rolls and gluing down the ends. When dry, pinch the rolls into teardrop shapes.

4 **Arrange the pieces and glue in place,** using the photograph as a guide. Glue staggered lengths of paper to the body and head so that the paper lengths stick up like "quills."

5 **Pinch, bend, and press** basic quilled circles and teardrops to make diamonds, triangles, and other shapes for clouds, flowers, animals, and other designs.

Quilling paper is just pretty paper that comes in ⅛-inch strips. Put any paper through a ribbon paper shredder and you can use it to quill!

Actual size: About 1 by
1 ³/₄ inches
Designed by: Colleen Lemons

RIBBON BOWS

Fabric bows are a simple way to get festive and fancy. Attach them to jewelry blanks, hair clips, and headbands for quick, dainty accessories to adorn jackets, hats, shoes, or you.

SUPPLIES

2 kinds of decorative ribbon

scissors

hot glue gun *and* glue stick

embroidery thread

pin back *or* alligator hair clip

1. **Cut 1 ribbon** into a 4½-inch-long piece. With wrong side facing, fold the ends to overlap about ¼ inch. Secure at the center of the overlap using a small dot of hot glue.

2. **Gather the bow** by laying about 6 inches of embroidery thread flat on a work surface. Center your folded ribbon on top, folded-in ends facing up. Tie the thread around the center of the ribbon and gently tighten. Secure the gather with a double knot and cut off excess thread.

3. **Cut a short length** of the remaining ribbon and use a dot of glue to attach one end to the pin back or clip. Then use another dot of hot glue to attach the center-back of the bow to the pin back or clip. Allow the glue to dry completely.

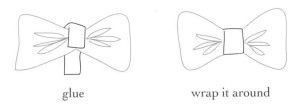

glue   wrap it around

4. **Apply a thin bead of hot glue** along both sides of the bow's cinched thread. Wrap the ribbon tightly around it and secure the ribbon to the back of the pin back with a dot of hot glue. Trim excess ribbon. Gently adjust and fluff the loops of the bow.

Any ribbon will do, but decorative 1-inch-wide styles in velvet, appliqué, grosgrain, and sequins will hold a stiff, desirable shape. Just avoid cutting through glitter, beads, and other decorations, which can cause unraveling.

Actual size: 1 ½ to 2 inches wide
Designed by: Sarah Goldschadt

SPEECH BUBBLES

Talking pie, cake, hamburgers—whatever!—are fun. Stick these speech bubbles into anything that's got something to say for itself.

SUPPLIES

tracing paper
pencil
scraps of card stock or thick paper
markers or a printer
scissors
tape or glue
toothpicks

2 **Add commentary!** The sky's the limit, but here are a few ideas to get you started:

Happy Birthday!

I ♡ You.

please don't eat me!

Vive la France!

$ax^2 + bx + c = 0$

Surprise!

Does this bun make me look fat?

it isn't easy being delicious.

Oink, oink!

1 **Trace patterns** onto the tracing paper and cut out. Use the ones below (or the free downloads available from quirkbooks.com/microcrafts). Then trace (or print) the patterns onto card stock and cut out the shapes.

3 **Tape or glue toothpicks to the back of each speech bubble.** Stick them into party food and let your treats do the talkin'!

SPOOL DOLLS

Kokeshi are small Japanese-inspired dolls that are traditionally made by painting hair and a face onto wood using a few simple lines. Turn spools of thread into these sweet little toys by using wooden beads, paint, and a bit of ribbon.

SUPPLIES

1 1-inch wooden ball or wooden bead

Small wooden spool (typically 1 $\frac{3}{16}$ by $\frac{7}{8}$ inches)

paintbrushes

satin varnish

craft paint

strong bonding glue

2 round wooden beads (8 mm is a good size), for hair buns

1 3$\frac{1}{2}$-inch piece of $\frac{1}{2}$-inch-wide ribbon

1 3$\frac{1}{2}$-inch piece of $\frac{5}{8}$-inch-wide ribbon

1 9-inch piece of $\frac{1}{8}$-inch-wide ribbon

hot glue gun

1 **Glue the wooden ball** to your spool with strong bonding glue and set it aside to dry. Paint the whole doll with satin varnish to seal the wood. Let it dry. Paint on eyes, nose, and mouth.

2 **For doll with hair buns,** draw 2 dots on the back of the head for placement and use a toothpick to apply bonding glue to dots and wooden beads. Stick beads to glue dots and tape or hold in place until dry.

3 **Paint the hair** however you like; blunt bangs are easiest. Keep it simple or add details, like flowers, hearts, hair clips, or butterflies. Dip the tip of the paintbrush handle in pink paint and touch it to the cheeks for blush.

4 **Varnish the face** with one quick brushstroke (too many swipes with the paintbrush will smear the marker). Let dry completely. Varnish the rest of the doll head, hair, and face one last time. Let dry completely.

5 **To make a kimono,** layer the medium ribbon in the center of the wide one. Tack them together with a dab of hot glue. Wrap the ribbon kimono around the spool and attach it with hot glue. Tie the narrow ribbon around it and make a bow in the front.

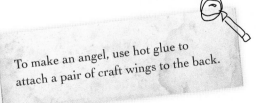

To make an angel, use hot glue to attach a pair of craft wings to the back.

Actual size: 1½ by 2 inches
Designed by: Mel Sparkles

TEDDY BEARS

For those days when you wish you could carry your teddy with you—but don't want strangers to stare—here are miniature bears so small they fit into matchboxes. (It's okay. No one will ever know.)

SUPPLIES

tracing paper

disappearing fabric marker

scissors

scrap of felt

seed beads

sewing thread *and* needle

embroidery thread *and* needle

polyester fiberfill for stuffing *or* felt, cotton, *or* yarn scraps

thin ribbon

1 **Trace the bear pattern** onto the tracing paper and cut out. Then trace the pattern twice onto the felt and cut out the shapes, just inside the marked lines.

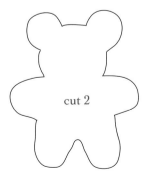

cut 2

2 **Give your bear a face.** Make eyes by sewing on seed beads or embroidering 2 French knots. Use embroidery thread to stitch a tiny nose.

3 **Use tiny stitches to sew** together the front and back pieces of the bear's body, with wrong sides facing. Leave an opening for stuffing.

4 **Gently stuff** with fiberfill or fabric scraps. Sew the opening closed. Tie a ribbon bow around the bear's neck (to make him extra cute).

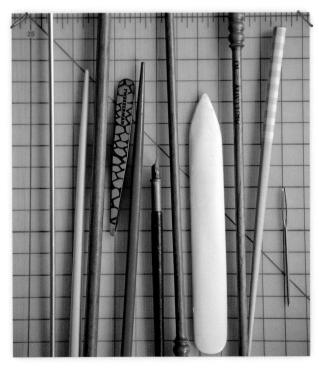

Patience is required when stuffing tiny craft projects—as is a good tool. Tweezers, toothpicks, crochet hooks, knitting needles, and skewers all work well.

Matchbox Bed

It's a bear in a box!

SUPPLIES

matchbox
craft paint
small paintbrush or toothpicks

Matchbox Bed

1 **Decorate the matchbox** using paints and brushes or toothpicks. You can photocopy the template below, attach it to the box, and paint it.

portrait template

Matchbox Blanket

1 **To knit a coverlet for your bear,** here's a simple pattern. With U.S. size 1 knitting needles and size 10 crochet thread, cast on 14 stitches. Knit 31 rows. Bind off.

2 **To crochet an itty-bitty blanket,** complete the following: With U.S. size 1 crochet hook (1.25mm) and size 10 crochet thread, ch 12. Sc for 16 rows. Finish off.

Nail-art paintbrushes found at the beauty-supply store work nicely for painting in miniature.

Other ideas:

- Make a fancy frame by dotting the paint in an oval shape.

- Trace the bear sewing pattern onto the box front and color it in with paint or markers. Add a protective coat of varnish to your painting, if desired.

- Glue fabric to the matchbox exterior and cut a matching blanket to fit inside (see Monsters Babies, page 49).

- Make a collage on the box front using a picture of a bear or a forest scene clipped from a book or magazine. Embellish with stickers or sequins.

Don't know how to knit? Simply fray the edges (as on page 50) or use a blanket stitch (page 83) to sew around the edges of a tiny scrap of fabric—easy!

Actual size: varies
Designed by: Alicia Kachmar

TEMPORARY TATTOOS

Only the most careful observers will notice a pony-shaped beauty mark on your face or a raccoon crawling across your foot! But your mom has eyes like a hawk. With these temporary tats, you won't risk being disowned. Getting inked is easy — and painless! —when special decal paper is put to the task (see page 85).

SUPPLIES

digital images

inkjet printer

office paper

clear temporary-tattoo inkjet waterslide-decal
 paper

adhesive sheets

scissors

sponge *or* cloth

1. **Print your images** using an inkjet printer and plain paper as a test run. When you're satisfied with how they look, print the images on the glossy side of the decal paper. Print 1 sheet at a time to avoid jams.

2. **Allow the ink to dry fully,** about a few minutes. Remove the clear side of the adhesive sheet and apply it to the printed decal paper. Cut around each tattoo design.

3. **Ink yourself!** Choose a spot for your tiny tattoo. Remove the adhesive backing from the decal paper and apply it to your skin, pressing firmly for about 20 seconds. Use a sponge or cloth to wet the paper for 60 seconds and then peel away the paper to reveal the design.

If you have a scanner and photo-editing software, you can scan these images or create your own designs.

Actual size: 1 ½ by 2 inches
Designed by: Len Kachmar and
Alicia Kachmar

THISTLE BIRD FEEDERS

Sometimes inspiration comes in the craziest places. Alicia's dad once remarked, "Every time I'm in a restaurant I think, 'These straws would be perfect for mini thistle feeders.'" The rest is history. If you're a bird lover, you'll never look at drinking straws the same way again!

SUPPLIES

¼-inch-diameter clear drinking straw

scissors

hole punch

cardboard scrap

craft glue

toothpick

pin

thick stiff silver wire

thin wire

small amount of black sand

needle-nose pliers

silver metallic paint

small paintbrush

1 **Cut the straw** to about 1½ inches long. Use the hole punch to cut 2 circles out of the cardboard and then trim one so that it'll fit snugly into the end of the straw. Set them aside.

2 **Put the smaller piece of cardboard** inside the straw about ⅛ inch from the bottom. Glue it in place by dipping the end of a toothpick in craft glue.

3 **With a pin, poke a hole** straight through both sides of the straw about ⅜ inch from the bottom. Poke a second set of holes perpendicular from the first set and about ⅝ inch from the bottom. Cut and insert two ⅛-inch pieces of thick wire into both sets of holes.

insert the wires

4 **Poke a third set of holes** about ¼ inch from the top of the straw, parallel to the bottom sets of holes.

5 **Cut a piece of thin wire** 1½ inches long. About ⅛ inch from one end, bend the wire 90 degrees using needle-nose pliers. Insert the wire into one of the holes at the top of the straw and bend the rest of the wire to insert it into the other hole. Crimp the wire flat against the straw using the pliers.

6 **Fill the feeder with sand** to within ⅜ inch from the top. Glue the remaining cardboard circle from step 1 onto the top end of the straw. Apply silver paint on the ends of the feeder. Allow to dry.

Tiny funnels are easy to make out of paper. They're great for filling micro-crafts with sand, glitter, and little beads.

Actual size: 2 ¼ inches wide
Designed by: Jessica Trail

YELLOW POLKA-DOT BIKINI

This swimsuit is so itsy-bitsy and teeny-weeny that it fits most dolls and little stuffed animals, too. (The elastic waistband is forgiving.) You can also hang the top from a keychain or wrap it around a cold bottle of Corona. It's time for a mini vacation!

SUPPLIES

tracing paper

pencil

1 8-by-5-in piece of yellow polka-dot fabric

1 8-by-5-in piece of lining fabric

pins

scissors

ribbon scrap

sewing machine *or* needle *and* thread

iron and ironing board

³⁄₄ in of hook-and-loop tape *or* snaps *or* button

4 in of ¹⁄₄-in-wide elastic

safety pin

2 **Cut the ribbon** to appropriate lengths for your doll or toy. Pin the ribbons to the top of the polka-dot piece and sew them on. Pin this piece to the lining, right sides facing, and sew the top and bottom seams, using a ¹⁄₄-inch seam allowance. Turn right-side out and iron flat.

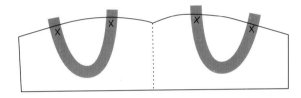

sew ribbon between layers of fabric

3 **Gather the center of the bikini top.** Set the sewing machine to the loosest stitch setting and sew a straight line down the center. Tie a knot in one end and pull the bobbin thread while pushing the fabric along the thread; knot the end. Hem the center back on both sides and stitch on hook-and-loop tape for closure.

Bikini Top

1 **Trace the pattern** onto the tracing paper and cut out the shapes. Then, placing the dotted edge on the fold, trace the pattern onto the polka-dot and lining fabrics, pin in place, and cut out.

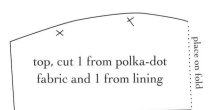

top, cut 1 from polka-dot fabric and 1 from lining

place on fold

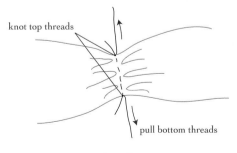

knot top threads

pull bottom threads

gather the top

Bikini Bottom

1 **Trace the pattern** onto the tracing paper twice and cut out the shapes. Then trace pattern onto the polka-dot and lining fabrics, pin in place, and cut out.

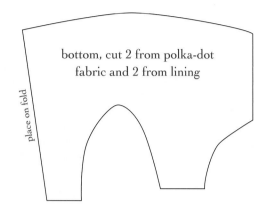

bottom, cut 2 from polka-dot fabric and 2 from lining

place on fold

2 **Pin the polka-dot fabric to the lining,** right sides together, along the top and leg openings. Sew the top seam and both leg openings. To prevent the fabric from bunching as you sew, clip the curves or cut notches about ¼ inch apart along the curved seam. Turn right-side out and iron flat.

sew top edge and leg openings, then turn right-side out

3 **Make a casing for the elastic** by sewing about ¼ inch from the top edge. Attach the safety pin to one end of the elastic and use it to tug the elastic through the band. When one end of the elastic lines up with the center back, double stitch to sew it down. Pull the other end of the elastic to the other side of the center back, and sew it down the same way.

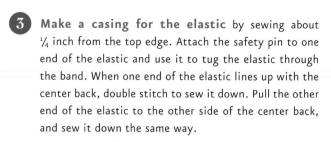

thread elastic through casing and sew down at center back

4 **Sew the complete center back** (both curved and straight parts) and crotch seams. Let's hit the beach!

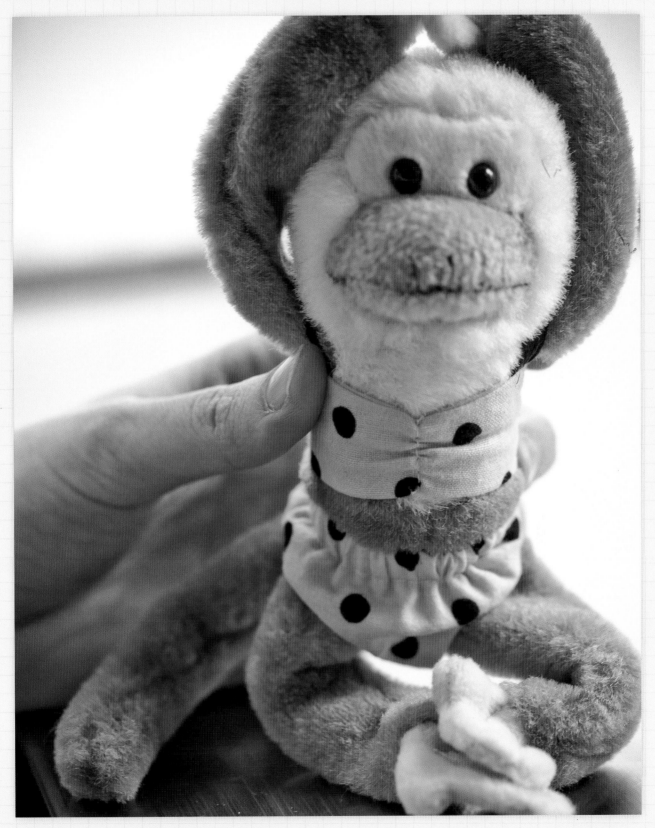

If you're making this bikini for a critter with a tail, leave an opening when sewing the center back seam. It'll be much more comfortable than using a leg hole.

Supplies *and* Techniques

You don't need expensive supplies for crafting on a miniature scale, just a few good tools and materials, plus a resourceful way of looking at what you find in your rag bin or thrift store. Here are our favorite supplies for working with tiny sewing patterns and little paper projects.

Brushes

Brushes of various sizes come in handy. Nail-art brushes available at beauty-supply stores are extra small and perfect for painting on tiny designs.

Button Cover Kits

These kits come in many sizes: 1/2 inch and 1/4 inch are best for microcrafting purposes. Use the cardboard from the kit box to trace the buttons and cut out circles of fabric for your buttons or button earrings. Snip off the button backs or buy flat-backed button cover kits if you want to adhere them to stud earring posts.

Card Stock

Also known as pasteboard or cover stock, card stock is paper that's thicker and more durable than usual. You can buy it new or recycle it if you've got old postcards, business cards, index cards, or playing cards.

Clear Nail Polish

Clear nail polish seals crafts and gives them a shiny finish.

Craft Knife

A craft knife (such as the X-Acto brand) makes it easier to cut around small patterns. You can gently touch the tip of the blade to tiny pattern pieces to pick them up when you're having trouble grabbing them with your fingers. A few tips for success:

• Always use a new, sharp blade.

• Use on top of a cutting mat—or a thick, sturdy piece of cardboard taped to a table—to keep things from slipping around and to protect your work surface.

• Keep your nondominant hand out of the path of the blade and keep pressure on the blade straight up and down to avoid unintended bevels or slippage.

• Gently sand slightly jagged cardboard edges with a bit of sandpaper.

Doll Accessories and Figurines

Barbie shoes and model-railroad figures are some of our favorite little toys. Use little accessories and other mini objects to dress up your microcrafts or attach them to jewelry blanks for quick micro-accessorizing.

Look for HO-scale railroad people—they're the perfect size.

Freezer Paper

Available in grocery stores and online, this paper is great for making craft patterns and stencils because it's a thick, heavy sheet that's coated in plastic on only one side, unlike wax paper, which is waxy on both sides.

Glue

Craft glue (a. k. a. white glue or tacky glue) is a good multi-purpose adhesive that's water based so it dries clear. Gel glue is ideal for paper projects, especially delicate paper and tissue paper. Bonding glue or epoxy (such as E-6000) is better for thicker materials and wood. A hot-glue gun is a trusty tool to have around for attaching all types of materials: It melts a solid stick of glue that dries as it cools.

Use a toothpick to apply small beads of adhesive to microcrafts without risking a giant glue blob emergency.

Jewelry Blanks

Available in a wide variety in craft stores and online, jewelry blanks are great for modifying microcrafts. Try earring studs, dangly earring hooks, rings, brooch pins, necklaces, and more. Attach an eye pin or a loop of thread to your craft if you need to make a hoop for dangling.

You can attach almost anything to a jewelry blank with a hole punch or a dab of craft glue.

Magnet Tape

You can find magnets in strips or coils. Simply cut a piece the size of your craft, peel off the backing, and press the sticky side onto the back.

Markers

Felt-tip markers work well for tracing little patterns onto scraps of felt and other fabrics. Disappearing fabric markers and dressmaker's pencils make it even easier. Permapaque markers are good for drawing on wood or other natural materials.

Matchboxes

These make good containers for tiny treasures. And you can decorate them with paint, fabric, sequins, or other supplies for a personal touch (pages 50 and 70). Cut off the match heads and you can use the matches like you would toothpicks in miniature projects.

Natural Materials

Natural materials like twigs, branches, and leaves are perfect for microcrafts. Objects like pebbles and pretty seashells you've been saving are fun to arrange in mini terrariums.

Polymer Clay

Polymer clay or modeling clay is fun to play with and can be shaped into almost anything. Possiblities abound!

Punches

A standard paper punch is good for making holes for gift tags and more. The leftover paper circles are fun for confetti or use in other projects. Larger-circle paper punches come in handy for projects that require bigger dots. Metal punches make it easy to knock holes out of metal for jewelry hooks.

Quilling Needle

This slotted needle makes it easy to quickly curl tiny strips of paper. You can use an embroidery needle with a big eye instead.

Recyclables

Save bottle caps, cardboard, paper, fabric scraps, and more in a bin. Then throw a microcrafting party!

Ruler

Any type will do. We recommend tape measures because they're flexible and metal rulers because they're good for cutting against to keep your craft knife straight and steady.

Sewing Machine *or* Needle and Thread

Either will work for microcrafts. When your stitches will show, try using embroidery thread instead of regular sewing thread for a prettier finish.

Mini Pattern Making

Patterns are helpful with all sorts of miniature crafts. There are a number of ways to make them.

- **Lay tracing paper** over templates like the ones in this book, trace the image, cut it out, and then trace it onto paper or fabric.

- **Scan and print images** onto regular paper or freezer paper and then cut them out and trace them to transfer the images to your crafting material.

- **Resize normal patterns** on your computer to shrink them to microsize.

Tiny Sewing Techniques

By hand or with a machine, microsewing isn't as hard as it looks. Here are the basic hand-sewing stitches we like to use for microcrafts.

Invisible ladder stitch

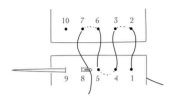

An easy way to close up seams and finish stitching up plushies after you've stuffed them.

French knot

Use this stitch for dots and eyes.

Whipstitch

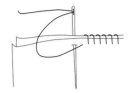

An easy and attractive stitch for small projects like tiny teddy bears.

Blanket stitch

This is a glorified whipstitch great for sewing up edges with a pretty finish.

Running stitch

Just a straight stitch. Easy peasy.

Satin stitch

Create a solid shape using a series of close parallel stitches.

Scissors

Small, pointy craft scissors or embroidery scissors are helpful when microcrafting since they're designed to cut with greater precision. Regular shears will work in a pinch.

Tape

Clear packing tape is good for laminating small pieces of paper, providing a waterproof seal. Pretty patterned tape provides a decorative finish. However, glue tends to be best when working small.

Toothpicks

These come in handy as tools and as craft supplies: You can use them to dab on paint (like mini paintbrushes) or cut them into pieces to make masts for miniature boats. Note that you may prefer round or square toothpicks, depending on the project.

Tracing Paper

Use tracing paper to transfer the patterns in this book—or to design your own. Transferring patterns onto card stock makes them sturdier and easier to trace. See page 82 for more info.

Tweezers

Picking up and placing tiny pieces is much easier with a good pair of tweezers. They're also helpful when stuffing little crafts.

Velcro

Perfect for wall mounting microcrafts like Deer Heads and Bottle Cap Frames.

Wire Cutters

Wire cutters are great for snipping pieces of wire. They're also better than scissors at trimming small wood pieces like twigs and toothpicks down to size.

Ideas for Modifying Microcrafts

You can adapt the instructions in this book to make your own miniature crafts into jewelry, toys, mobiles, installations, and more.

Accessories and Jewelry

Attach microcrafts to jewelry blanks for rings, necklaces, and earrings. Or use them to modify barrettes, hair ties, and headbands or bookmarks, key chain fobs, and cell-phone charms. You can even stitch or pin them onto purses and tote bags or your favorite pair of mittens.

Turn tiny books into jewelry charms: Just insert a jump ring or a loop of string into the book end before gluing on the cover.

With a dab of craft glue and needle-nose pliers, it's easy to attach almost any craft to a jewelry blank . . .

Even a houseplant!

Decorations

Use microcrafts to add a little something special to your décor at home, in the office—or even in a public space for someone to discover.

Leave little surprises tucked into funny places. Look for nooks in spice racks, shelves, cracks in brick walls. A good spot in your medicine cabinet will surprise nosy guests.

Hook tiny crafts onto suction cups to decorate windows. A loop of thread sewn or glued to the back makes any microcraft into a cute holiday ornament.

Letters

Fold microcrafts into mini envelopes or wrap them up in tiny boxes to stuff into care packages for friends. The tiny envelope pattern on page 41 can be resized (bigger or smaller) with the aid of a computer or copier. Fold small letters or delicate microcrafts (like the cats or ladybugs, bumblebees, or butterflies) inside. Just remember that the U.S. Postal Service won't deliver anything under the size of 5-by-3½ inches—you have to place it inside a larger envelope.

Magnets

Stick a magnet onto the back for decorating the refrigerator or other metal surfaces.

Mobiles

To make a mobile, cut the heads off two long match sticks or use dowel rods, BBQ skewers, or tree branches cut to length. Position like an X and wrap string or fishing line around the middle, knotting at the beginning and end and securing with glue.

Pins and Tacks

Glue microcrafts to pins and tacks and you can use them in cork boards or stick them straight into walls (if your walls are drywall and the homeowner approves . . .).

Presents

Now there's a use for pretty little pieces of wrapping paper that it's a shame to throw out. Save jewelry boxes and other little packages and wrap microcrafts up in festive paper tied with a bow. Miniature gift bows the size of a dime are available in most stores that carry regular-size wrapping paper.

The best presents come in the littlest boxes.

Resources

Here are some of our favorite sources for materials and tools.

A.C. Moore Arts & Crafts: acmoore.com

Addicted to Crafts: addictedtocrafts.com

Craftiest Craft Forum and Blogs: getcrafty.com

Create for Less: createforless.com

Cute Minis (tiny Japanese treasures): cuteminis.com

Decal Paper (for temporary tattoo paper): decalpaper.com

Denver Doll Emporium (doll and food miniatures including hard-to-find brands like Re-Ment): denverdoll.com

Dick Blick Art Materials: dickblick.com

Etsy: etsy.com

Factory Direct Craft: factorydirectcraft.com

Home at Paperchase: paperchase.co.uk

Jo-Ann Fabrics: joann.com

KnitMap (find your local yarn store): knitmap.com

Knitty magazine and store: knitty.com

Logee's Tropical Plants (including rare plants, succulents, and miniatures): Logees.com

Model Railroad Figurines and Supplies: hobbylinc.com

Michael's Craft Stores: michaels.com

Miniatures (dollhouse supplies): miniatures.com

The Papery Store: thepapery.com

Pearl Fine Art Supplies: pearlpaint.com

Priscilla's Treasures (Japanese miniatures for dolls and dioramas): nrfbqueen.com

Utrecht Art Supplies: utrechtart.com

About *the* Authors

The crafters and designers featured in this book live across the United States and favor a variety of different mediums and methods, but we all share a love of miniature handicrafts. Please visit our blogs and websites to ask us microcrafting questions or just to say hello.

A big fan of all things miniature, **Margaret McGuire** is an editor at Quirk Books. She lives in South Philadelphia.

If you're fast enough to pin down **Alicia Kachmar**, you'll find her crocheting up a storm on Etsy (eternalsunshine.etsy .com), teaching classes, or stocking the Craft-O-Tron machine in Pittsburgh, Pennsylvania.

A designer, seamstress, and all-around handywoman, **Katie Hatz** wears many hats—and has a remarkable tolerance for hat puns. Check out her work at katiehatz.com and buy her wares at katiehatz.etsy.com. She lives in Philadelphia.

At Barker's Herbs and Heirlooms, **Tamara Barker** crafts miniatures and steampunk works that combine upcycled materials with her fondness for Victorian aesthetics and design. You can find her at barkerbell.etsy.com and at home in Pittsburgh, Pennsylvania.

A flea-market and thrift-store junkie, **Claudia Cormier** is always hunting for that one special treasure to use in a new creation, whether it's furniture, pictures, tea cups, fabric, buttons, or jewelry. A resident of Kansas City, Missouri, Claudia sells her crafts at howbeadyful.etsy.com.

Elizabeth Duke loves making tiny yet detailed jewelry and quilling paper embellishments for her toddler son's scrapbook at home in East Liverpool, Ohio. She can be found at destashlife.etsy.com.

A dedicated crafter and designer, **Sarah Goldschadt** finds inspiration in Scandinavian design. Her website is sarahgoldschadt.com, and her shop is goldylocks.etsy.com.

Larissa Holland loves teeny things. Peruse her blog at mmmcrafts.blogspot.com and browse her shop at mmmcrafts.etsy.com. A resident of Atlanta, Georgia, Larissa is addicted to all things artsy and craftsy. And coffee.

With an MFA in book arts and printmaking and a job as the production and sales coordinator at Quirk Books, **Melissa Jacobson** is an expert at making books, large or small. Her work can be found at ISOthers.org. She lives in an appropriately tiny apartment in Philadelphia.

Parents of microcrafter Alicia Kachmar, **Len and Melaine Kachmar** are always ready to tackle the next craft project, whether it's miniature birdfeeders or felted planets.

On a mission to reduce, reuse, and amuse, **Holly Keller** lives in Minneapolis, Minnesota, where she makes dolls and plush crafts out of other people's unwanted stuff. Visit her blog Chez Beeper Bébé (chezbeeperbebe.blogspot.com) and shop (beeperbebe.etsy.com).

The woman behind the handcrafted fashion and wedding Shop at No. 144, **Colleen Lemons** is a graphic and interior designer who blogs at mrslemons.wordpress.com. She resides in Phoenix, Arizona.

Specializing in mini sweets and snacks, **Mei Pak** has been crafting customizable food jewelry since 2006. Find her eye-candy designs at tinyhandsonline.com.

Known for her dioramas and micro-mini tiny kitties, **Mel Sparkles** sells tiny handmade gifts, toys, collectibles, and other goodies at sparklerama.etsy.com. She loves to make tiny toys and dollhouse miniatures.

Jessica Trail was inspired to become a seamstress by her mother, who made her all sorts of little toys and doll clothes. Jessica lives in Jacksonville, Florida, and is the proprietor of Trail's Crafts (trailscrafts.etsy.com).

Hope Watthanaphand is an enthusiastic crafter who has been creating art since she was young. She loves the spontaneity of trying new types of arts and crafts, which she sells at hopesartcreations.etsy.com. She lives in Ohio with her easy-going husband and four children.

Nadia Marks Wojcik is an artist and crafter working primarily with paper. She works as a nanny and a full-time creator of things for her online shops Ready Go Paper Studio and Oh, Hello There. A Pittsburgh resident, she is inspired by paper and all of its possibilities and, of course, cake.